T0003203

DAMAGED
BUT NOT
DESTROYED

STUDY GUIDE

DAMAGED
BUT NOT
DESTROYED

STUDY GUIDE

FROM **TRAUMA** TO **TRIUMPH**

MICHAEL TODD

No book can replace the diagnostic expertise and medical advice of a trusted health care professional. Please be certain to consult with your provider before making any decisions that affect your health, including your mental health, particularly if you suffer from any condition or have any symptom that may require treatment.

2023 WaterBrook Trade Paperback Original

Copyright © 2023 by Michael Todd

All rights reserved.

Published in the United States by WaterBrook, an imprint of Random House, a division of Penguin Random House LLC.

WATERBROOK and colophon are registered trademarks of Penguin Random House LLC.

Some material is adapted from *Damaged but Not Destroyed* by Michael Todd, copyright © 2023 by Michael Todd, first published in the United States by WaterBrook, an imprint of Random House, a division of Penguin Random House LLC, in 2023.

Trade Paperback ISBN 978-0-593-44491-7
Ebook ISBN 978-0-593-44492-4

The Cataloging-in-Publication Data is on file with the Library of Congress.

Printed in the United States of America on acid-free paper

waterbrookmultnomah.com

2 4 6 8 9 7 5 3 1

Most WaterBrook books are available at special quantity discounts for bulk purchase for premiums, fundraising, and corporate and educational needs by organizations, churches, and businesses. Special books or book excerpts also can be created to fit specific needs. For details, contact specialmarketscms@penguinrandomhouse.com.

CONTENTS

Introduction

3

SESSION 1

The Hit You Didn't See Coming

7

SESSION 2

Dang, I'm Damaged

17

SESSION 3

Say My Name

25

SESSION 4

Damaged and Still Good

33

SESSION 5

Damaged Is Not (Supposed to Be) a Destination

43

SESSION 6

Pull Up a Chair

53

SESSION 7

Say Ouch!

63

SESSION 8

When Damage Is an Inside Job

71

SESSION 9

Damage Control

81

SESSION 10

Designer Damage

91

DAMAGED
BUT NOT
DESTROYED

STUDY GUIDE

INTRODUCTION

This study guide is designed to work in a lot of different situations—including small groups, book discussion groups, or on your own as you walk through your healing journey. In any case, this book was created to be a companion to *Damaged but Not Destroyed,* where I share true stories and practical principles for everyone making the journey from hurt to healing.

We've all been knocked down, taken hits that have left us damaged in one way or another. The good news is, healing is waiting for you. But no one can heal *for* you. The damage you've experienced may not be your fault, but it is now your responsibility. Your healing can't happen without your participation.

So take a deep breath, commit to walking through this study guide with honesty and intentionality, and see how God shows up.

This participant's guide is a deep dive into the principles laid out in *Damaged but Not Destroyed,* with an emphasis on gaining wisdom from God's Word. The content here is structured for a ten-week study.

HOW TO USE THIS GUIDE

Start each session by reading a chapter in *Damaged but Not Destroyed,* and engage with the principles you discover there. Then jump over to this study guide, and begin applying those principles to your life. Read chapter 1 for session 1, chapter 2 for session 2, and so on.

Remember to allow yourself—and God!—the time and space to work on your heart and mind.

THE GROUP EXPERIENCE

God didn't design human life to be lived alone, and that goes double for life in the Spirit. The healing journey is best taken together, so if possible, I encourage you to find a couple of friends to walk with you. We need other Jesus people to help us live a Jesus-shaped life.

This guide will work best in a group setting if you personally walk through each session a day or two before you meet so that you can spend your time together in discussion. Each session includes enough material for about forty minutes of meeting time, though you can adapt the length to your group's needs. Whether you are the group leader or a participant, be kind, sensitive, and respectful of the other people in your group. Healing is hard! It isn't always linear, and each person's journey has its ups and downs. Do all you can to create a place of safety and love so that everyone can receive what the Spirit is so ready to give.

SESSION FORMAT

Each session includes three sections:

1. *Let the Word In.* Read, meditate, and reflect on a passage of Scripture. We English speakers read Scripture in translation rather than in the original languages (Hebrew and Greek). So try reading the same passage in a few different Bible translations to get a deeper feel for and fuller picture of what God is saying through the original writers. Some go-to translations are the New International Version (NIV), the New Living Translation (NLT), and the New King James Version (NKJV).

2. *Let the Truth Out.* Practice being H.O.T. (humble, open, and transparent) with yourself and God. Sit with each question, and let it guide you in identifying the damage you've experienced. This might bring up some discomfort—even pain— because the hits hurt. But pay attention to the pain spots because they will show you what is ready to be healed. And as much as you are able, share your thoughts and insights with the people in your group.

3. *Let the Spirit Guide.* Pray through the thoughts, feelings, and issues that come up for you throughout the study. Let the Holy Spirit guide you and heal you. Lasting restoration involves God's Spirit helping us understand our own damage in a new way. His healing puts our damage in context so it becomes part, not the whole, of our story.

BE H.O.T.

In this study, we're going to dive deep into the way God restores damaged people to His original design. We're going to get real about self-discovery and healing together, but in order to do that, we've got to commit to being H.O.T.—humble, open, and transparent about our damage.

Real healing isn't about saving face or trying to look cool. There's no need to hide. God wants to heal your damage—no matter how bad, how deep, or how ugly—and bring you into your destiny.

So I urge you to commit now to being humble, open, and transparent with yourself, with God, and with those around you. Because when you're ready to be real, you're ready to heal.

This journey is incredibly worth every bit of work because receiving God's healing will transform your life, your relationships, and your faith in the most important ways.

Ready?

Let's go.

THE HIT YOU DIDN'T SEE COMING

BASED ON CHAPTER 1 OF *DAMAGED BUT NOT DESTROYED*

As we go along in life, our relationships, circumstances, and choices inflict damage that won't heal with an ice pack. Hits leave bruises on our minds, bodies, and souls. These hits come whether we expect them to or not. They're inevitable. Unavoidable. Predictable, even. Many times they leave us looking a mess. Our thoughts and feelings are fragmented and disorganized. Our physical, financial, and vocational health are limping along on life support. From the outside perspective, we look destroyed.

But here's good news for you: What's inside you—your true gift, your spirit—can't be destroyed by outside damage, because your spirit was handcrafted by God in His own image.

Please hear this: No matter what happened to you, no matter who hurt you, no matter how hollow you feel . . . *the value is still in you.*

LET THE WORD IN

Read Psalm 139:1–18, out loud if possible. Explore a few Bible translations to get a fuller picture of what God is saying in this passage.

After you've finished reading, sit quietly for a minute or two. In our crazy, loud, busy, hyperconnected world, being quiet is a radical act that helps us make space for God. Don't check your phone! Just be here, right here, where you are.

As you read Psalm 139, what feelings come up in you? Assurance? Disbelief? Hope? Fear? Anger? Write them all down, even if they're mixed up or conflicting. Note which lines in the psalm provoke a particular feeling in you. (For example, verse 7 might inspire calm or anxiety in different people.) Take five to ten minutes with this exercise. The goal is to get an accurate inner temperature reading when it comes to your belief in the value God has placed inside you.

LET THE TRUTH OUT

1. In chapter 1, we learned about a few different kinds of damaging hits. Which ones have you experienced? Write down a few details about each hit you've taken.

The Dumb Hit: *I did it to myself.*

The Distracted Hit: *I didn't see it coming, because I was looking the wrong way.*

The Delayed Hit: *So ferocious that I couldn't feel it until later.*

The Direct Hit: *Straight-up sin that I couldn't or can't escape.*

The Disaster Hit: *A widespread event that affected everyone around me.*

The Disguised Hit: *I thought it would be a blessing, but instead, it knocked me on my butt.*

The Domino Hit: *A knockout punch that began an unstoppable chain reaction toward hopelessness.*

Other Hits: *Anything and everything not covered by the definitions above.*

2. When you think about the hits you've taken so far in your life, which have made the biggest or most lasting impact? Why do you think that is?

3. Which areas of your life have been most affected? Which areas are top priority for you when it comes to healing? Why?

4. Dealing with our past pain, our present problems, and the fight for our future will get messy. But it's so incredibly worth it.

How do you feel about the healing adventure you're starting here? Nervous? Excited? Skeptical? Is it easy or hard to believe that it will be worth it? Why?

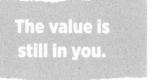
The value is still in you.

Most of us have a hard time believing we have value, especially when the metaphorical gift of our lives—our covering and container—has been kicked, cut, bleached, torn, and torched. But anchor yourself in this truth until you know it way down deep in your bones:

Your contents—your spirit, your core, your eternal essence—were handcrafted with love and purpose by the Creator of the universe.

Your value is so significant that once you understand who God has made you to be, it becomes power to achieve victory in every circumstance. Your value is for victory.

5. When you imagine victory in every circumstance of your life, what might it look like? Be honest with yourself and God. He may want to tweak or transform your definition of victory, but that can happen only if you're H.O.T. (humble, open, and transparent).

LET THE SPIRIT GUIDE

Take a few deep breaths. If you would like to write down thoughts as you go along, you can use the "Notes" section that appears at the end of each chapter.

Recognizing the damage that has shown up in our lives is hard work. As much as you might want to jump to problem-solving, don't try to fix anything yet. Just practice being aware of the damage and turn your attention to God's presence with you in the pain and discomfort.

LET'S PRAY

Holy Spirit, I believe that You are with me.

Or at least, I want to believe it.

*Give me courage to face the damage of my
past and the new hits I take each day.*

*Help me respond in faith instead of
fear, trusting that I'm not alone
on this adventure.*

*I want to know You and live the destiny You
planned just for me.*

Amen.

NOTES

2

DANG, I'M DAMAGED

BASED ON CHAPTER 2 OF *DAMAGED BUT NOT DESTROYED*

Jesus tells us, "In this world you will have trouble" (John 16:33). The thing about trouble is that it's usually traumatic. But the greater tragedy is undealt-with trauma.

If you're real enough to admit that you feel like, "Dang, I'm damaged"—because of the mistakes you've made, because of the goals you haven't reached, because of the violations you've endured, because you're still dealing with things you thought you'd be over by now—know that you're in good company. Let this sink in: You're not alone.

Be encouraged. The current state of your damage does not determine the deliverance you can experience.

LET THE WORD IN

Read 1 Timothy 1:12–17, out loud if possible. Check out a few different Bible translations to gather more insight into the full meaning of this passage.

After you've finished reading, sit quietly for a minute or two. Remember, being quiet is a radical, countercultural act that helps us make space for God. Don't check your phone!

> When we understand the pattern, we can pinpoint the problem.

Just be here, and let God's Word settle in your heart.

This letter to a young pastor named Timothy was written by the apostle Paul, one of the people personally appointed by the risen Jesus to spread the good news of God's kingdom. Based on this section of his letter, how would you say Paul feels about the damage of his past? Is it similar to or different from how you feel about your damage? In what ways?

LET THE TRUTH OUT

1. Let's define *damage*. We all get hit, but not every hit leaves a mark, right? So let's agree that what we're talking about when we talk about damage is *what hits and sticks*, like on a dartboard. If the dart bounces off or misses altogether, there's no damage. But if it's thrown at just the right angle from just the right distance with just the right velocity and force, *thonk*. Bull's-eye. You've got damage.

How well does the image of a dartboard resonate with you as you try to understand how damage happens in your life?

Can you think of hits you've taken that *didn't* stick, that just kind of bounced off and didn't leave a mark? Why do you think they didn't hit the target of your heart? How were they different from the bull's-eyes?

2. You've been dodging darts from birth. These are the aerodynamic weapons fashioned by your adversary (Ephesians 6:16) that are aimed at your purpose, whether you know it or not. From living rooms to classrooms, bedrooms to boardrooms, courtrooms to dorm rooms—everywhere we live our lives, darts are flying and their assignment is damage.

Do you find it easy or hard to believe that you have an enemy, the devil, who means to harm you? Why would you say that is? How could knowing about him help you make sense of the damage that has been done to you?

3. As you get to know Mephibosheth (nicknamed Phibs), what feelings does his story provoke in you? Pity? Scorn? Camaraderie? A little bit of each, or something else entirely?

4. Is how you feel about him similar to or different from how you feel about damaged people you know personally? Or how you feel about yourself? Why do you think that is?

5. Once you've worked on a few equations of "Math with Mike" (pages 40–42 of *Damaged but Not Destroyed*), journal a few lines here about what thoughts and feelings rise up in you as you try to make sense of damage in this way. You might feel uncertain or confused. You might feel fresh grief or relief. Where do you think those feelings are coming from?

LET THE SPIRIT GUIDE

Remember, damage isn't all God-*caused,* but all of it can be God-*used.* Our Creator doesn't let anything go to waste! This week, take a few minutes at the end of each day to give thanks for God's intention to use your damage for good. You may not be able to see it yet, but your damage is an indispensable aspect of your God-created destiny.

Tap into your imagination and begin to envision what that destiny might be. Jesus told His disciples, "With God all things are possible" (Matthew 19:26). If that's true (and it is), what might it mean for you?

LET'S PRAY

*God, it's sometimes hard to believe that
You can make something good out of
all this damage.*

*Help me trust You to do Your work
while I do mine.*

*Keep me focused on remembering the
hits and revealing to myself and to
You where it hurts.*

*Thank You for healing me, even though
I don't feel it yet.*

Amen.

NOTES

SAY MY NAME

BASED ON CHAPTER 3 OF *DAMAGED BUT NOT DESTROYED*

It's all but impossible to heal damage that we're not aware of—especially when we cope with our damage in a way that looks good from the outside. Unless we look closely, it doesn't look like damage at all.

Have you ever seen someone with incredible drive to succeed but that drive is their way of running from something?

Have you ever seen someone who makes everybody laugh but the jokes are a cover to keep from crying?

Have you ever seen someone whose life looks perfect but something tells you it's an exhausting attempt to maintain control?

Not everything that appears good about our personality comes from a good place. It may be rooted in rejection. Or it may be rooted in disappointment, neglect, insecurity, or shame. But it's imperative for each of us to discover the root of our behavior, because whatever drives us will determine our destination.

We need to discover what drives us.

LET THE WORD IN

Read Philippians 3:4–11, out loud if possible. Remember to explore a few Bible translations to get a fuller picture of what God is saying through this passage.

After you've finished reading, sit quietly for a minute or two and let Scripture settle in your heart.

This letter to the Christians in a city called Philippi was also written by the apostle Paul (remember him from last session?). Based on this passage, what drove Paul before he met Jesus? What is driving him now?

Some people experience a dramatic and immediate transformation when they encounter Christ's restoring power. In fact, Paul's conversion was so sudden and dramatic, people were like, wait, what?! *Isn't this the guy who was hunting down Jesus followers and arresting them five minutes ago?* By contrast, other people find themselves changing more gradually over time. How have you noticed Christ restoring your motivations and desires? How do you see your priorities shifting or reordering? In what areas of your life do you wish you could see more dramatic changes?

LET THE TRUTH OUT

1. Everybody copes with damage in different ways. Sometimes coping mechanisms are unhealthy straight out of the gate—like substances or habits to numb the pain or an overreliance on aggression to defend against perceived threats. But more often they are adaptations that seem to benefit us, at least for a little while.

How have you adapted to your damage in ways that appear to be or maybe even feel beneficial? Does knowing this make it harder or easier to want to change? Why?

2. When God designed you, He installed a dashboard with all kinds of lights and sounds to help you keep tabs on the health of your vehicle of value. But much like your car's dashboard, it's useful only if you pay attention to it. If you ignore flashing lights and warning bells long enough, you become desensitized to the very indicators that are meant to keep you safe.

Some of us can't see or hear the warnings anymore—until the day we offer someone a ride. Our damage indicators are more evident in relationships. We're more likely to notice the check-engine light that's been blinking red for too long when there's someone in the car with us.

Give some thought to your past relationships. When has a person close to you helped bring your damage into the open (intentionally or not)? When have you brought someone else's damage to the surface through your relationship with them (intentionally or not)?

3. Why do you think relationships are so effective at bringing damage to light?

4. It's hard to admit we need help, so let's practice. All together now:

> I.
> NEED.
> HELP.

Help from the right people in the right context brings healing. James 5:16 says, "Confess your sins to each other and pray for each other so that you may be healed. The prayer of a righteous person is powerful and effective."

Who in your life might be walking with you toward healing? Keep in mind that who these people are might be surprising, like the friend who tells it to us straight, the pastor who challenges our assumptions, or the spouse or sibling who knows our potential.

5. Think back to the times people helped you move toward healing. What did they say or do that helped the most?

LET THE SPIRIT GUIDE

This week, think and pray about your relationships. Whether with your significant other, parents, kids, extended family members, friends, neighbors, or co-workers, each relationship can be a place of healing or of further damage—and sometimes both! Spend a few minutes praying about one person in your life. Ask God's Spirit to reveal to you how your damage is affecting the health or frailty of the relationship, and how their damage may be affecting you. Pray God's blessing on them, that His will would be done in their life and that He would show you how to be an agent of healing for them.

Your healing is hidden in help.

LET'S PRAY

*Thank You, God, for putting other
humans in my life.*

*I know it's not good to be alone—even though
sometimes it feels like that might be easier!*

I want to honor You in my relationships.

*Show me how You are already at work in the
lives of those around me.*

*Help me not to get in the way but instead to
follow Your lead in blessing, healing,
and loving.*

Amen.

NOTES

DAMAGED AND STILL GOOD

BASED ON CHAPTER 4 OF *DAMAGED BUT NOT DESTROYED*

The only thing worse than being damaged is allowing your damage to multiply in the lives of the people you love most. If you're tired of doing the work only for yourself, consider the next generation of your family. Please don't pass your wounds on to the people who matter most to you.

Your healing isn't only for you.

Toxic generational cycles are a real thing.

But here's good news: *Transformed* generational cycles are a real thing too.

What if we could be the pivot points for our entire family lines? That may sound too big for one person, but God's Word tells us that a good man or a good woman "leaves an inheritance for their children's children" (Proverbs 13:22).

When most of us hear that scripture, we think of financial security and wealth. But what if the inheritance God is referring to also includes health? Emotional health. Spir-

> **Your decision for healing can change destinies.**

itual health. Soul health. Communication health. Relational health.

What if the work we're doing right now could result in a rewarding treasure of transformation for our family?

Your decision for healing can change destinies.

LET THE WORD IN

Read Psalm 22:22–31, out loud if possible. Explore a few Bible translations to get a fuller picture of what God is saying through this passage.

After you've finished reading, sit quietly for a minute or two. Remember, being quiet is a radical, countercultural act that helps us make space for God and His Word to speak into our lives.

As you read Psalm 22, what feelings come up in you? Hope? Disbelief? Thankfulness? Fear? Anger? Write them all down, even if they're mixed up or conflicting. Note which lines in the psalm provoke a particular feeling in you. (For example, verse 24 might inspire hope or skepticism in different people.) Take your time with this exercise. The goal is to take your heart's temperature when it comes to a desire to pass faith, trust, and wholeness on to future generations.

LET THE TRUTH OUT

1. We pass our unhealed wounds on to our children. We can't help it. Generational cycles are a tragic statement of fact, as we see in the Bible (Exodus 20:4–6; 34:6–9). "The sin of the parents" shapes us. Their unhealed damage turns into darts that end up poking holes in our wholeness.

Where do you see negative generational cycles at work in your life? What damaging behaviors, attitudes, tendencies, or temptations did you inherit from your family? How many generations back does the damage go?

2. Let me give you a picture of what God has planned for you.

My brilliant mother, in addition to being a gifted preacher, is a wizard in the kitchen. A dented can? A torn label? A broken box? The more damage, the better. It was a challenge! She loved to show that something beautiful could come from something broken. Brenda Todd knew that even if the container was damaged, the value was still in there—and she was going to find it. She'd pile those raggedy-looking products into her cart, take them home, have her boys carry them inside, and then work her magic. When she was done, our family would sit around the table like we were in one of those heartwarming Hallmark scenes and feast on a meal that was *chef's kiss*.

In my mother's masterful hands, what was once considered damaged became delicious. Not only that—the discounted contents also became a valuable blessing to the people who needed it most.

Spend some time thinking about the value of *you*. It may feel weird or arrogant or self-involved at first, but try it. Yes, the damage is real. But the value is still in you. And not just generic "everybody's valuable" value, but value that God has put *only* in you.

What is your unique value? Think about what you've been called to bring into His world.

If you're not sure where to start, consider what natural gifts you bring to your relationships and your work. What do people experience when they're around you? If you're still not sure, ask a trusted friend or spiritual adviser, such as a small-group leader or pastor, to help you identify your purpose and gifts.

Write down your unique value. Be as specific and detailed as you can.

3. God will use your damage to accomplish your destiny. That's why guilt, shame, and condemnation are so dumb. Ain't nobody got time for that. Whether the damage wasn't your fault or you are totally, completely, solely to blame—or, realistically, a little bit of both—drowning in shame isn't what God wants for you or from you.

How does shame show up in your life? Is it a feeling you struggle with frequently, sometimes, or not very often?

4. What situations, words, thoughts, or feelings tend to stir up shame in you? What events or seasons from your past is that sense of shame connected to?

5. Some families, communities, and even churches use shame to motivate people (especially young people!) to make positive choices for their lives. What are some alternative ways to motivate one another?

LET THE SPIRIT GUIDE

This week, put your guilt and shame front and center. Remember, God won't heal what you don't reveal! Bring it all into His light, and talk it through with Him. He already knows, so just let it all hang out.

Paul wrote to the Christians in Rome, "There is no condemnation for those who belong to Christ Jesus. And because you belong to him, the power of the life-giving Spirit has freed you from the power of sin that leads to death" (Romans 8:1–2, NLT).

Did you hear that? *No condemnation.* None. Zero. This is a condemnation-free zone, so air out that dirty laundry and allow God's Spirit to give you a fresh start. Write it all down, pray it all through, and invite God to heal you.

LET'S PRAY

Sometimes shame eats me up inside, God, and keeps me from living in full, perfect freedom.

I want to be free from the power of shame!

So today, right now, I'm letting Your light shine in.

Help me know down deep that You don't condemn me, and please help me stop condemning myself.

I want to live in Your light and love.

Amen.

NOTES

DAMAGED IS NOT (SUPPOSED TO BE) A DESTINATION

BASED ON CHAPTER 5 OF *DAMAGED BUT NOT DESTROYED*

The story of Mephibosheth and King David is a picture of our relationship with the real King. If Mephibosheth is a shadow of us and if King David is a shadow of Jesus, there is good news for you, my friend: You are on the King's mind.

Maybe you feel more paralyzed and purposeless than ever before. You are on the King's mind.

You may be barely scraping by, without one red cent to your name. You are on the King's mind.

Are you trapped by a physical ailment, bound by your body's limitations? You are on the King's mind.

Or perhaps you're blocked by mental illness or unhealed emotional trauma, tricked into desolation by a mind that needs restoration and renewal. You are on the King's mind.

Whatever your Lo-debar is, whatever you're doing or

> **Think about that!** *God* in all His God-ness has *you* in all your you-ness on His mind.

not doing, you are topmost in the King of the universe's thoughts.

In other words, you are on the King's mind.

If you're like Phibs, lying there helpless and hopeless in your metaphorical Lo-debar, it's almost impossible to believe you're on God's mind. That's understandable. But that doesn't make it less true.

LET THE WORD IN

Read John 18:15–18, 25–27, which recounts events that took place in the hours leading up to Jesus's execution; then skip over to John 21:14–19, which records a conversation that happened after His resurrection. Read the same passages in another translation or two to deepen your understanding of these texts.

After you've finished reading, sit quietly for a minute or two and think on the verses.

Peter was a disciple of Jesus who eventually became one of the leading apostles the Holy Spirit used to spread the good news of Christ. But before that happened, Peter lied about even knowing Jesus because he was afraid for his own life. Can you imagine the mixed emotions he must have felt when he saw the risen Lord on that beach? Using your holy imagination, put yourself in his sandals for a few minutes. How would you have felt? Ashamed? Excited? Afraid? Hopeful?

Write about those feelings, and try to identify the root of each. Where is the shame coming from, for example? What about the hope?

LET THE TRUTH OUT

1. Do you think you're safe from grace—the unearned, undeserved kindness and favor of God our King? Sorry to disappoint you! Our King has a tracking device of unconditional love on you. You can run, but you cannot hide.

Have you ever tried to hide from God's pursuit of you? Maybe you're doing it right now. What did you do to try to stay off God's radar?

2. Why did you want to hide? Is knowing that you're unconditionally loved by God reassuring or a little scary—or a bit of both? Why?

3. Yes, damage is frequently caused by people. But that same damage is healed through people. For some reason, God chooses to use imperfect, damaged people to do His perfect work of restoration. So for any of you who have vowed never to let people close to you again or who believe you're better off by yourself, wrap your mind around this one: Your healing is in someone else's hands. The King will send people into your life to carry you emotionally, spiritually, and even physically to a new place that you can't get to on your own.

How does this idea feel to you? Does it sound more like good news or bad news? Why?

4. It's God's will for us to rescue and restore damaged people. Remember "Hurt people hurt people"? It's also true that healed people heal people.

Let me really blow your mind, though: Damaged people (that's all of us!) can help heal people.

Every phone call to express concern, every "just checking on you" text message, every shared tear, every milestone celebration, every challenging and encouraging conversation, and every time of prayer are the real-life, practical ways we carry damaged people to the King.

Which scenario freaks you out more: You being carried to

the King by others, or you helping carry someone else into God's presence? Why?

Do you think it's possible to do both in a healthy and godly way? How?

5. Who in your life needs help getting to the King? Who does the Spirit bring to your mind? What kind of help can you offer that both honors their free will—as God does—and maintains your healthy emotional boundaries? (If you're not sure what that would look like, talk with a trusted friend, a spiritual adviser, or a mental health professional.)

LET THE SPIRIT GUIDE

This week, pray about how helping others could be a healthy part of your own healing—not an excuse to avoid your own spiritual and emotional work, but rather an opportunity for you and others to draw closer to God. Ask the Holy Spirit to reveal how He wants to work both in you and in other people. And as you go about your activities during the next week, keep an eye open for how God might be speaking to you, healing you, and caring for you through the people around you.

LET'S PRAY

*God, I want to be healed and
to be a healer.*

*Please show me how to do both without
doing more damage to me or
to anyone else!*

*Your ways are higher than my ways,
and I trust You to show me the
path forward.*

Amen.

NOTES

PULL UP A CHAIR

BASED ON CHAPTER 6 OF *DAMAGED BUT NOT DESTROYED*

Regular silence and solitude are among the most radical, countercultural spiritual practices we can engage in today.

I've always been loud, big, flashy, and extra. I thrive on intensity. In fact, before I began the work of healing, I would create intensity when I felt like there wasn't enough. I would ramp up the drama and raise the stakes to *juuuuuuuuust* below everybody's breaking point and would love every minute of the adrenaline rush.

My wife, Natalie, is the opposite. She thrives on peace, space, and quiet, which I used to routinely, thoughtlessly disrupt. A couple of years ago, she asked me, "Why are you like that?" And instead of getting defensive and angry, I decided I actually wanted to know the answer. Why *was* I like that? It was a question that made me uncomfortable, but rather than running away from the discomfort, I decided to just kind of sit in it.

Maybe I don't need to say it, but up to that point, silence did *not* play a big part in my spiritual life. So I began to dip my toe into being quiet. It felt foreign. Weird. Uneasy. Pointless. Dumb. Awkward. Difficult.

After about a week of (mostly uncomfortable) quiet time

with God, my mind finally got quiet too. I ran out of thoughts to distract myself and ran into real silence. I could finally Hear.

I could finally Hear Him.

And I was ready to listen.

LET THE WORD IN

Read Isaiah 30:15–21, out loud if possible. Read these verses in a few different translations to get a fuller picture of what God is saying in this passage.

After you've finished reading, sit for a minute or two in the quiet. Don't check your phone! Just be here, right where you are.

The prophet Isaiah tried to warn God's people about an invasion by a foreign nation called the Assyrians and to advise them on how to respond: Get quiet. Rest confidently in God. But read verses 1–2 and notice what they did instead: They fled, and they sought help from others!

As you reflect on your own life patterns, what is your go-to response when you're facing stress or calamity? What is your first impulse? Why do you think that is?

LET THE TRUTH OUT

1. You may be out of Lo-debar, but Lo-debar isn't out of you. If you're like me, you've been living in Lo-debar for as long as you can remember. And it sure looks like there is no escaping these habits. For some of us, our old way of thinking is our only way of thinking. I want to let you know, I feel you.

What we're calling Lo-debar has just been life for many of us. If somebody makes us mad, we want to fight. If somebody hurts us, our cutoff game is strong. We're used to doing whatever makes us feel better in the moment: drink or pills or porn or shopping or golf or french fries or a busy schedule—it doesn't matter. When we feel afraid or ashamed, we want to hide or run away or lie to protect ourselves. All we know is Lo-debar.

What habits, impulses, behaviors, or attitudes in your life are distracting you from getting quiet, getting still, and getting honest about what's going on?

2. What efforts, whether positive or negative, have you made to get rid of the distractions? For example, are you actively forming healthy habits to deal with what's distracting you? Or are you just trying to ignore and suppress what's really going on? Be honest with yourself: How is it going?

3. Our hearts get buried under our relentless quest for achievement, affirmation, security, status, or any number of other things. But when we learn to H.U.S.H., God helps us excavate our hearts. And that's when the real healing can begin.

Hear from God
Allow your **U**nderstanding to progress
Share intimately in a safe space
Get to the **H**eart of the matter

Psalm 34:18 says, "The LORD is close to the broken-hearted; he rescues those whose spirits are crushed" (NLT).

Let me give you the passage remix: God is drawn to hurting hearts and scarred spirits. God leans close to tattered trust and insecurity issues. God longs to keep company with damaged people who are discouraged and dejected. We've got to H.U.S.H.

Which step of H.U.S.H. comes most naturally to you? Which is hardest? Why is that? What small action can you take to practice the hardest part of H.U.S.H.?

4. I'm being as literal and straightforward as I know how to be: Get in the King's presence. The way to healing? It's in the King's presence. The wisdom you've been searching for? That's there too. The inner confidence in who you are as a child of God? Yeah, you'll find that in the King's presence.

One way I get into God's presence is with something I like to call the Thirsty Thirty:

Ten minutes of reading the Bible
Ten minutes of prayer
Ten minutes of worship

This is how you practically pull up a chair at His table and get in His presence so that you can Hear from Him.

What habits like the Thirsty Thirty are you cultivating that regularly put you in the King's presence? What spiritual habits do you wish you had? Take a minute and identify small, attainable steps to create a rhythm of getting into the King's presence. And if spending time in the King's presence is already a daily discipline for you, don't let yourself off the hook. Think about how God is inviting you to go deeper and listen better during that time.

> Hearing the truth of your inner experience is a choice.

5. Zoom out for just a minute to assess how you feel at the prospect of regular, intentional quiet time in the King's presence. Phibs probably wasn't thrilled at the idea—he may have even felt like his life was in danger! It's okay to feel afraid, angry, ashamed, or whatever. Write down the emotions you notice and why you think they've shown up. Your emotions don't have to make your decisions, but you do need to be aware of them so they don't take charge behind the scenes and keep you from spending time with God.

LET THE SPIRIT GUIDE

This week, pray for yourself and the people around you. Specifically, pray that each of you will begin to experience life outside of Lo-debar as you cultivate the habits of life in the King's presence. Ask for deliverance and freedom in everyone's life, including yours. As you spend time interceding for each person, pay close attention to any words of encouragement, insight, or healing that the Holy Spirit might give you for that sister or brother. Write them down and then deliver the message!

LET'S PRAY

King Jesus, I want to live full-time in Your presence, but my past keeps showing up in my thoughts, words, and deeds.

Replace the habits of my Lo-debar with spiritual disciplines that keep me close to You.

Help me help others get free, too, Lord.

Thank You for always inviting us to sit at Your table of grace.

Amen.

NOTES

SAY OUCH!

BASED ON CHAPTER 7 OF *DAMAGED BUT NOT DESTROYED*

We all need to express emotions. Why? Because God designed feelings to come out, not to fester inside. If we lock them down instead of letting them out, our emotions will eat us alive from the inside. Unexpressed emotions turn to dis-ease or disease.

If we don't outwardly express sadness, disappointment, and grief, they turn inward and fester into depression.

If we don't outwardly express fear, worry, and doubt, they turn inward and fester into anxiety.

If we don't outwardly express frustration, violation, and pain, they turn inward and fester into rage.

Science tells us that many physical sicknesses are linked to emotional illness.* If that's true, could our emotional healing be an antidote for our physical ailments?

I locked my vulnerability in a vault when I was really young. It's been only a few years since I found the combination, but opening the door that I thought was protecting me

---

* See, for example, "How Does Mental Health Affect Physical Health," WebMD, March 29, 2021, www.webmd.com/mental-health/how-does -mental-health-affect-physical-health.

When grace drops in, God restores generational blessings.

has proved to be one of the most valuable gifts I could ever give myself. I started to use the power of words for healing.

When was the last time you said ouch? Because it's only when you're vulnerable enough to admit you're hurt that you're vulnerable enough to get healed.

LET THE WORD IN

Read Psalm 38, out loud if possible. Remember to explore a few Bible translations to get a fuller picture of what God is saying through this passage.

After you've finished reading, sit quietly for a bit, letting your mind and heart process the scripture. Keep that phone down. Just be present to the Word.

What feelings come up for you when you read this ancient poem? Does its raw realness make you a little squirmy? Why? Do you feel relieved or reassured that it's okay to acknowledge negative emotions and experiences? How do you imagine God responding to David's complaints?

LET THE TRUTH OUT

1. Your next step toward healing is to take a snapshot of your current condition. It's time to recognize the hurt.

Don't freak out. Please don't try to cover up your scratches, dents, dings, and damage. C'mon, we're past that.

We need to be *real* for our "before" picture. No filter.

We need to take an inventory of everywhere it hurt.

It might surprise you, but in a very real sense, the "Your 'Before' Pictures" exercise in chapter 7 is a modern-day version of Psalm 38. Compare how you felt doing the exercise with how you felt reading the psalm. Did you experience some of the same emotions? Or were the two experiences different? Why do you think that is?

2. Why is saying ouch so hard for so many of us? What holds us back? What are we afraid of? And how does this reluctance to say ouch influence our journey toward healing?

3. There is a blessing God intended for your parent, grandparent, or great-grandparent that has been waiting for someone in your family to step up and say, "I'll take that." You might have thought it was lost forever, but just because the people before us fumbled their blessings doesn't mean that God did.

Have you ever considered the connection between recognizing the hurt (saying ouch) and being able to receive the blessing God intends for you and your family? How can acknowledging your wounds prepare you to claim what God has stored up for you?

4. Sometimes the damage in our lives and in our family causes us to view God-given generational gifts with distrust or disgust. Because of how we've seen those gifts used or not used, we may find it uncomfortable that we share a talent or characteristic with a family member. But God wants to restore those blessings. What generational gifts have you suppressed? What would it look like to receive them as gifts from God?

5. Jealousy is a gateway sin. When it takes over your imagination, you eventually find yourself in places you never thought you'd be, doing things you never thought you'd do, chasing things that were never yours to begin with. First jealousy, then selfish ambition, and the next thing you know, you're boasting, lying, manipulating, and up to your eyeballs in evil of every kind.

Jealousy is something everybody struggles with at one time or another, but that doesn't make it any less dangerous to your heart and mind. When was the last time you felt that little green monster rear its ugly head? What did you do? Are you satisfied with how you responded? What would you do differently next time?

LET THE SPIRIT GUIDE

This week, practice recognizing your hurts without trying to *feel* better. The feeling-better part is coming—promise! But for now, practice saying ouch to yourself and to God.

Psalms are a great place to start, because the book of Psalms is filled with laments, gut-level honesty, and raw vulnerability. In particular, check out Psalms 35, 42, 55, 56, 57, 64, 69, 70, 102, 108, and 139. In fact, try praying some of those psalms— the same ones that God's people have prayed and sung throughout the centuries and around the globe—and discover for yourself that our King isn't troubled in the least by our heartfelt expressions of grief, anger, pain, and sadness.

LET'S PRAY

Holy Spirit, show me how to be real with You.

I don't want to pretend anymore.

I'm wounded, God.

I know that You know.

*But give me courage to say out loud,
to myself and to You, the specific
hurts I'm carrying around.*

Help me reveal so that You can heal.

Amen.

NOTES

WHEN DAMAGE IS AN INSIDE JOB

BASED ON CHAPTER 8 OF *DAMAGED BUT NOT DESTROYED*

Isn't it funny how easy it is to see the toilet paper stuck on somebody else's shoe? How is it even possible that they don't know? Those three or four bright white squares are a silent billboard announcing exactly where they've been and what they've been doing. They're out here dragging a damp streamer of evidence behind them, and they have no idea.

Sometimes our damage is just like that: easy for everybody else to see and invisible to us.

I can relate. I have allowed unhealed damage to become a hindrance—not because I didn't care or because I was being reckless, but because I didn't know. I couldn't see. I didn't realize.

I didn't realize that my obsession with greatness would rob me of everyday joys.

I didn't realize that when I traded good for great, I would miss meaningful moments that I can never get back.

I didn't realize that demanding perfection from others would cut off their opportunity to grow.

> Wounds heal properly only when they are properly treated.

I didn't realize that idolizing the ideal would send me into isolation.

My obsession with greatness was an adaptation to damage that served me for many years in many settings—until it didn't. Until one day my wife asked, "Why are you like that?" and I realized my damage was a hindrance to my present and my future.

LET THE WORD IN

Read Acts 8:26–39, out loud if possible. Check out a few different Bible translations to gain a deeper understanding of the meaning of these verses.

After you've finished reading, sit quietly for a minute or two. Remember, being quiet is a radical, countercultural act that helps us make space for God. Don't check your phone! Just be here, right where you are.

Philip was one of Jesus's original eleven disciples who received the Holy Spirit (Acts 1–2) and obeyed the Lord's Great Commission (Matthew 28:16–20) to spread the gospel of Christ. Because of his witness to this Ethiopian man, the Christian faith spread to Ethiopia, and the church has been there ever since. But consider the Ethiopian we meet in this passage. Did you notice that everything he says is a question? Rather than pretending he knows the answers or trying to fake his way through the conversation, he is completely open about the gaps in his knowledge that are hindering him from understanding God's Word.

As you consider your own life, what would it look like to take your cue from this early Christian convert and get curious? How might you change if you became more willing to admit your ignorance, pain, or shortcomings and ask questions? What do you think you could learn about yourself, others, and God?

LET THE TRUTH OUT

1. If you could be the Ethiopian man from today's Bible passage for just a few minutes, what questions would you ask about the Scriptures, about Jesus, or about living life with God?

2. Many families today allow the domino effect of dysfunction to divide and devastate them every holiday season. Shoot, forget holidays. There's drama every time the family gets together! Sharp darts—words, actions, environment, and exposure—get hurled at the people we're supposed to love. And inevitably, even though they may not show it, somebody gets damaged. We know there are problems. We know there is pain. We can feel the pressure—but nobody talks about it! It's business as usual, like nothing ever happened.

Sound familiar?

Why do you think dealing openly with family dysfunction is so hard? For you personally, what person or situation is the most challenging to respond to in a healthy way? Why?

3. If you're like me, self-sabotage isn't your goal—but correcting it is now your job. You're not consciously trying to undermine your relationships, creative pursuits, career, and future success. But now you've got to take responsibility to realize the hindrance.

Does this feel like good news or bad news? When it comes to taking responsibility for how your damage hinders your life and purpose, do you feel more hopeful or fearful? Why?

4. Review the story in "A Prototype of Progression," starting on page 137 of *Damaged but Not Destroyed*. Is there an event, season, or assignment that you've been ignoring or trying to forget because the result was disappointing? Give yourself permission to revisit it, maybe with a trusted friend who knows you well and whose insights are godly and reliable. How did your damage hinder you from appreciating its value at the time? What value did you miss by trying to shut it down or shut it out?

5. Even if that experience seems, by all accounts, a failure overall, what good might God accomplish through you because of it?

LET THE SPIRIT GUIDE

This week, ask God's Spirit to alert you when your damage is hindering your purpose, relationships, or future. Snap a picture of your completed "The Enemy's Lies, My Creator's Eyes" table on page 141 of *Damaged but Not Destroyed*. When you sense that you're speaking a lie to yourself, refer to the picture and remind yourself of the truth. Then allow God to reframe your thinking, and move forward in trust that He wants to show you how to view yourself and your circumstances through His eyes.

LET'S PRAY

*Creator God, I don't want to make choices
based on the Enemy's lies.*

*But I need Your help to renew the way
I see myself.*

*Please help me stop allowing my damage
to be a hindrance.*

*Give me eyes to see and ears to hear Your
truth, and courage to act on it.*

*And with each new action, help me
form fresh habits.*

Amen.

NOTES

DAMAGE CONTROL

BASED ON CHAPTER 9 OF *DAMAGED BUT NOT DESTROYED*

I travel a lot, and on the rare occasion that I'm early for my flight, I love to watch people whose plane is about to leave race to the gate. It's hilarious. If you're flying commercial and you're late, you better run. I mean *run*. It doesn't matter who you are, how much money you make, how much you weigh, how many people you're traveling with, your ethnicity, or the last time you worked out: When those boarding doors are about to close, you better run, Forrest, run! If you care more about looking cute or like you have it all together, you're gonna miss your flight.

Sometimes it's worth losing your dignity to get to your destination. I confess, I have more than once had to lose my cool to make my connection.

Mephibosheth gets this concept. Instead of the smart play, he makes the faithful play. He doesn't care about looking foolish; he cares only about keeping his connection with the king (2 Samuel 19). He gets humble. He takes the low road.

I'll be real with you: This is a hard one for me, but maybe not in the way you'd think. The hardest thing isn't being H.O.T. (humble, open, and transparent) about the stupid, sinful stuff I've done—porn addiction, premarital sex, car insur-

> **The greatest reward of bringing your damage to God is getting to know your Designer.**

ance fraud, etc.—because I know the Enemy is defeated by the blood of the Lamb (grace) and the word of my testimony (Revelation 12:11). Talking about my failures keeps me accountable and keeps the devil defeated!

What's hard for me is being vulnerable. Looking weak. Saying ouch. I wish I could be strong and proud and cool and still get healed, you know?

But it's just not possible. Healing isn't about looking cool.

LET THE WORD IN

Read Matthew 26:57–68, out loud if possible. Read it in a few different translations to get a fuller picture of what God is saying in this passage.

After you've finished reading, sit for a minute or two in the quiet. Don't check your phone! Just be here, right where you are.

After Jesus is betrayed by one of His own disciples, Judas, He is put on trial by a council of religious authorities called the Sanhedrin. They accuse Him of blasphemy, saying false things about God, which is a crime punishable by death under their law. But instead of defending Himself, Jesus submits to their judgment and punishment. Here's the thing, though: He doesn't submit because they are right. He submits because He is being obedient to His Father's will. (Read verses 36–46 of this chapter.)

Have you ever been falsely accused? How did you handle the situation? It's certainly not always wrong to defend ourselves—but it's not always right or wise either. Based on how Jesus and Phibs handle themselves, what do you think are some good guidelines for deciding which response is called for?

LET THE TRUTH OUT

1. When my kids make a mess or a mistake, they run *to* me, not *away from* me. They don't hide. They want Daddy's help. "Daddy, help!" is yelled or whispered or sobbed at least daily in the Todd house, and then I'm handed something stained, sticky, broken, inoperable, or all of the above. My kids are not afraid to tell me when they mess up, and they're not afraid to ask me to fix it. Humility is natural when there's trust, and my children trust me.

Around the same time I realized that my reluctance to be vulnerable was a hindrance, I also realized that I didn't trust God the way my kids trust me. Instead of running to the Father the minute I got damaged by others or myself, I would try to sort it out on my own and then present Him with a solution. I told myself I was helping God, as if that's possible.

What is your first impulse when damage happens? Be honest! What do you do first when everything is going wrong? Why do you think that is?

2. Take another look at the blanks you filled in for "The King Knows Best" on page 151 of *Damaged but Not Destroyed*. Which would you say is the easiest and which is the most difficult when it comes to trusting the King to know best? Why? What is one truth you can practice saying this week to remind yourself that God is trustworthy in this area?

3. The greatest reward of bringing your damage to God isn't that He will heal you (although that's pretty amazing). The greatest reward of bringing your damage to God is getting to know your Designer.

I promise, this is what you'll discover after significant time living in the King's household and basking in His presence: He is worth more than all of it put together. More than loving family relationships. More than financial security. More than mental and emotional health. More than life-giving intimacy in marriage. More than success and influence. More than purpose.

I honestly believe that all those blessings and more are what our Designer has in mind for us and that He's ready to pour them out when we are ready to receive them. But I also *know*, after walking with the King for a good while now, that the purpose of those blessings is to draw us deeper into the Source of them all.

When you look at all the demands and opportunities in your life, where does closeness with the King come in? Where would you like it to be? Go ahead and rank your priorities in the space below. Only honest answers will help you out here—so be H.O.T. (humble, open, and transparent). Remember, humility makes room for the Holy Spirit.

4. What would have to shift in your daily schedule for you to draw close to the King's presence regularly? Sometimes we might need to recruit our family, roommates, or friends to help us find creative solutions.

5. God is with us wherever we go. He's with us in whatever we're doing. How might you practice being with God even while you're going about your day?

LET THE SPIRIT GUIDE

Spend a few minutes praying through the "Lord, You Know Best" list on page 172 of *Damaged but Not Destroyed*. As you pray over each item on the list, notice the "buts" that come up in your thoughts and feelings, as in, "I trust You, but . . ." Go ahead and write all of them down, and then ask God to give you faith to trust Him—not *in spite of* the buts, but *through* them. You don't have to ignore your worries, concerns, and doubts, or pretend they don't exist. You can be real with your Designer—no ifs, ands, or buts.

LET'S PRAY

My King, I want to trust You. But it's hard!

I feel afraid. I feel anxious.
I feel unsettled and skeptical.

Teach me how to trust You.

I need assurance of Your love so that
I can take baby steps of faith.

Show me what it looks like to trust
You in all things.

Amen.

NOTES

DESIGNER DAMAGE

BASED ON CHAPTER 10 OF *DAMAGED BUT NOT DESTROYED*

I don't believe God causes damage, but I believe He uses it. What happened to me as a thirteen-year-old drummer who wanted to play in big church—He didn't cause it. But receiving His healing for that wound has convinced me that for our Designer all damage is usable material. He didn't cause the rejection, but through the healing process, He turned my obsession with greatness into obedience and gratefulness. He didn't cause the abuse I experienced as a kid, the disappointments and challenges I had to navigate as an adult. But through the healing process, He drew me closer to Himself.

Complete deliverance can happen in a moment. I've seen addicts set free in a split second. I've seen terminal diagnoses turn around after one prayer. I've seen depressed people overcome with joy in worship.

But many times (maybe even most of the time), deliverance is gradual. It happens over time, under the radar, in the dark, behind your back when you're not looking. Sometimes you notice it only

The heavy lifting of healing is on Him.

after the fact, like when you make a different choice than you would have a year ago or when your response to something that used to set you off is surprisingly different.

Something's changed, you think to yourself. *Oh, wait. It's me.*

It's more than okay if you're not there yet, my friend. Please don't freak out. Trust the Designer and remember: progression, not perfection. Stay H.O.T. (humble, open, and transparent), and do the work—because that's when and how deliverance shows up.

LET THE WORD IN

Read Mark 5, which records three healing encounters with Jesus. Check out a few different translations to explore the full meaning of the passage.

After you've finished reading, sit quietly for a minute or two. Remember, being quiet helps us make space for God. Don't check your phone! Just be here, and let Scripture speak to your mind and heart.

In this passage, three people receive healing from Jesus *in three totally different ways.* What specific differences do you notice? What similarities, if any, do you see? Which person do you identify with most? Why?

LET THE TRUTH OUT

1. When I began to consistently choose good over great, I knew I had experienced God's healing. When you begin to experience God's healing, what changes do you think you will notice? What changes, if any, have you noticed already? As you experience more deliverance, what behaviors, attitudes, and assumptions do you think will be different?

2. The process of healing often takes months or years or decades, especially in the case of childhood trauma. But sometimes it can take only days or even hours, once we get in the habit of healing. That was my experience after "the spit hit the fan" (see chapters 5 and 10 of *Damaged but Not Destroyed*). Because of what I had learned through healing my teenage rejection and disappointment, I already was prepared for the process. It didn't make it easier, but I knew what to expect.

> Remember the hit.
> Recognize the hurt.
> Realize the hindrance.
> Reset to humility.
> Receive God's healing.

Take another look at the five R's above. Which step do you feel you're on right now? What are some ways you could follow this pattern the next time a hit lands on your life? Be specific and practical so that healing can become a habit.

3. We progress through the healing steps as much as we are able. But God is the healer, not us. He does the heavy lifting. What thoughts and emotions does this fact bring up for you? Relief? Worry? Comfort? Or the feeling of being out of control? Take a minute to think about why that is and write down your thoughts.

4. By the time I walked into church the week after the spit hit the fan, I knew I had begun receiving God's healing. It was confirmed in an unexpected way. Just before I walked out to preach, my brother Brentom wrapped me in a bear hug, which prompted me to do something I had never done before: break down in tears. Sobbing in his arms. Y'all, I ugly cried, gasping for breath, out of sheer gratefulness and relief. My response was the epitome of vulnerability and the exact opposite of what I would have done if I were still in an un-healthy space. That's when I knew I was safe. I was whole. I was healing.

Close your eyes, breathe deeply for sixty seconds, and let yourself notice the *feelings* of healing. As you reflect on both the healing you've received and the healing that's coming, what do you feel in your body? Do you feel tears coming up, like I did? Or maybe your shoulders start to release some tension. Pay close attention to your heart and body. As you slowly breathe in and out, what do you notice?

5. Psalm 147:3 says, "He heals the brokenhearted and binds up their wounds." Write that verse on a sticky note or two, and post them around your house, in your car, in your work space, or in other spots where they will catch your eye. Work on committing it to memory this week. God is your healer. Let the truth of His Word assure you!

LET THE SPIRIT GUIDE

Meditate in prayer on the image of a Venetian mirror, and take an inventory of your life's cracks, bubbles, and discolorations. Don't be quick to move from one flaw to the next; be willing to pause at each place of damage. As you contemplate the parts of your life, try to take a mental step back and ask God to show you how they each belong and work together in the masterpiece of your life. Then ask your Designer to give you a vision, even just a glimpse, of how He can use both your damage and your healing for His glory. Write it all down below (or on the "Notes" page for this chapter) so that you can return here in a few weeks, months, or years and give Him praise for all He has done and will do in your life.

LET'S PRAY

*Creator God, help me trust that, to You,
even my damage is usable material.*

*You can make beauty from these ashes,
a masterpiece from these cracks.*

*Give me a glimpse of the victories You can
win and the new life of wholeness You
make possible through my healing.*

I want to become who You created me to be!

*Show me how to let You shine bright
through my imperfections.*

Amen.

NOTES

ABOUT THE AUTHOR

MICHAEL TODD is the lead pastor of Transformation Church in Tulsa, Oklahoma, alongside his wife, Natalie. They were entrusted with Transformation Church by the founding pastor, Bishop Gary McIntosh, in 2015, after fifteen years of leadership.

Their personal philosophy and driving passion at Transformation Church is re-presenting God to the lost and found for transformation in Christ. They aspire to reach their community, city, and world with the gospel presented in a relevant and progressive way. You can find out more about Transformation Church at www.transformchurch.us.

Michael is also the multiple *New York Times* bestselling author of *Relationship Goals* and *Crazy Faith,* and each year he speaks at influential churches and conferences, such as Elevation Church, VOUSCon, XO Marriage Conference, Gateway Church, and others. Michael and Natalie have been married since 2010 and live in Tulsa with their four children: Isabella Monet, Michael Jr., Ava Rae, and Gia Joy.

You can find out more at
@iammiketodd and www.iammiketodd.com.

Discover the Value in You

Journey from tragedy to triumph with the powerful teaching and practical tools in bestselling author Michael Todd's book, *Damaged but Not Destroyed*.

Prefer to listen and learn?
Get the *Damaged but Not Destroyed* audiobook on your favorite audio app!